ONE-ROOM SCHOOLHOUSES
OF THE
MAHANTONGO VALLEY

STEVE AND JOAN TROUTMAN

an imprint of Sunbury Press, Inc.
Mechanicsburg, PA USA

an imprint of Sunbury Press, Inc.
Mechanicsburg, PA USA

Copyright © 2024 by Steve and Joan Troutman.
Cover Copyright © 2024 by Sunbury Press, Inc.

Sunbury Press supports copyright. Copyright fuels creativity, encourages diverse voices, promotes free speech, and creates a vibrant culture. Thank you for buying an authorized edition of this book and for complying with copyright laws. Except for the quotation of short passages for the purpose of criticism and review, no part of this publication may be reproduced, scanned, or distributed in any form without permission. You are supporting writers and allowing Sunbury Press to continue to publish books for every reader. For information contact Sunbury Press, Inc., Subsidiary Rights Dept., PO Box 548, Boiling Springs, PA 17007 USA or legal@sunburypress.com.

For information about special discounts for bulk purchases, please contact Sunbury Press Orders Dept. at (855) 338-8359 or orders@sunburypress.com.

To request one of our authors for speaking engagements or book signings, please contact Sunbury Press Publicity Dept. at publicity@sunburypress.com.

FIRST DISTELFINK PRESS EDITION: October 2024

Set in Adobe Garamond | Interior design by Crystal Devine | Cover design by Lawrence Knorr | Edited by Lawrence Knorr.

Publisher's Cataloging-in-Publication Data
Names: Troutman, Steve, author | Troutman, Joan, author.
Title: One-room schoolhouses of the Mahantongo Valley / Steve and Joan Troutman.
Description: First trade paperback edition. | Mechanicsburg, PA : Distelfink Press, 2024.
Summary: There are a multitude of one-room schoolhouse pictures. If you are from the Mahantongo Valley, you may find a name you recognize.
Identifiers: ISBN : 1-979-8-88819-246-7 (softcover).
Subjects: HISTORY / United States / State & Local / Middle Atlantic.

Designed in the USA
0 1 1 2 3 5 8 13 21 34 55

For the Love of Books!

Thank you and Dedication

A special thank you must be given to the late Marion (Romberger) Troutman of Klingerstown and Jack Leitzel of Hebe. Marion attended Noble School and may be seen as a student on page 27. Jack Leitzel attended Hebe School and may be seen as a student on page 19. Marion Troutman's photo collection and historical perspectives in combination with Jack Leitzel's one room school photos with location narratives, provided the impetus for this book. Many others contributed narratives and photos including Dennis Boyer, William Burkey, Dr. John Romberger, Shirley Silvick, Steve Scott, Mary Straub, Lawrence Maurer, Nancy (Hoffman) Rothermel, Marion Klinger, and John D. Troutman.

This book is dedicated to the above named historians and all others who strive to record our cultural heritage.

About the book cover art:
Bryant A. Troutman, son of George and Mary (Rabuck) Troutman, lived between Hebe and Klingerstown. Bryant attended Nobel School, locally named Rothermel's One Room School. Bryant commissioned Deanna Wiseman of Herndon to create an accurate representation of the school house and the surrounding scenery. The painting entitled, *Dinner Time Ball Game* was painted ca. 2007. By July 30, 2008, the painting was made available to the public in print form, as advertised in the *Citizen Standard* newspaper.
    Danelle Cavell, sister of the artist, composed and contributed the newspaper article entitled, "One Room School House Memories Preserved by Wiseman Print." Danelle's article captures very well, Bryant's remembrances of this school house.
    Deanna composed an enlightened scene, as a reminder of days gone by, and can be enjoyed by everyone today.

Table of Contents

Introduction: One-Room Schoolhouses in Jordan Township by Marion A. Troutman 1

PUBLIC SCHOOLS

1. Union School 3
2. Forest School 5
3. Grove School 16
4. Hebe School 18
5. Nobel (Rothermel's) School 23
6. Linden School 33
7. Urban School 34
8. Dubendorf (Gap) School 38
9. Troutman School 40
10. Paul's School 41
11. Stein's School 44
12. Fetterolf School 46
13. Delb-Delp School 48
14. Zerfing's School 51

About the Authors 54

INTRODUCTION

One-Room Schoolhouses in Jordan Township

by Marion A. Troutman

Jordan Township was formed on August 4, 1852, from territories previously of Jackson and Upper Mahanoy Townships. The township of Jordan was named after our first presiding judge of Northumberland County, who was elected by the people of the entire area. The region is drained by the Mahantongo Creek, emptying into the Susquehanna River, and also by the Middle and Mouse Creeks, which empty into Greenbrier and Fiddlers Run Creeks, which empty into the Susquehanna River.

The public schools in Jordan Township (one-room schoolhouses) were as follows:

- Union (Bohner's) – Located north of Union Cemetery at the intersection to Richard Troutman's farmstead. Homestead of two teachers.

- Forest (Lesher's) – Located west of Hebe on the road crossing the mountain to Urban. Now this school is the Hebe Church Community Center.

- Grove – Located between Klingerstown and Hebe, directly across the road from Ray and Mamie Kratzer's property.

- Hebe – After tearing down the Grove school, they build a school in the village of Hebe, known as the Hebe School. Some building material from the Grove school was used to build the Hebe School, now remodeled by James Troutman as his residence in Hebe.

- Nobel (Rothermel's) – Located between Klingerstown and Hebe. The teachers from Nobel's School were from a German background because many pupils starting school could not speak English. The teachers were as follows: Beatrice Rohrbaugh, Marlin Reed, Mrs. Marlin Reed, William E. (Cracker) Schlegel, William Troutman (father of Roscoe Troutman), Jacob C. Hoffman, Warren G. Leitzel, Beulah Wenzel, Molly Bowman, Ida Philips.

- Linden – Records have shown this early school located 1½ miles east of Urban. This school was near the former Ernest (Sunny) Long Residence. This building had been torn down long ago. Pupils were then sent to Nobel's or the Urban School. The school was discontinued due to not enough children in the area.

- Urban School – Located directly east of Urban Church. It is now the homestead of surveyor William Messner.

- Dubendorf (Gap) – Located in the small gap east of Mandata, near the old Meckley farmstead on the road leading into Raupstal.

Nevin Troutman stated that early private school was held in a building on the Troutman farm, now known as the Meeting House – Evan. Church Building. It had first been an early German school when public schools were started. The Troutman family started a church in the same building. This never was a public school.

The Meeting House was located at the intersection of Meeting House Road and Klingerstown Road, between Hebe and Pillow. The Meeting House was built as a schoolhouse in 1840. When the public schools were built in 1865, the building was converted to Troutman's United Evangelical Church. Church services were held there until 1920. After that, it was used as a storage shed until about 1970, when it was torn down due to road improvements.

The Meeting House, 1840–1919.

CHAPTER 1

Union School

Union School (1865–1958).

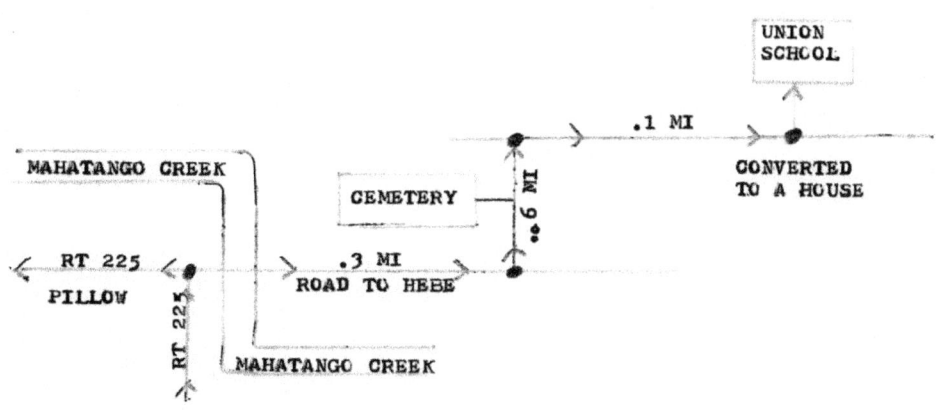

Union School, 1938.

Front row sitting (L to R): Daniel Ferree, Albert Hollenbach, Arthur Peiffer, Marlin Troutman, Albert Leitzel, Guy Hoffman, Melvin Smeltz, and Lawrence Bohner.

Middle row (L to R): Bill Hollenbach, James Leitzel, Dorothy Peiffer, John Troutman, Robert Leitzel, Bobbie Hoffman, Unknown Bahner, Delmar Wirt, Troy White, and Unknown Bahner.

Back row (L to R): Margaret Troutman, Gertrude Ferree, Polly Hollenbach, Hilda Hollenbach, Hellen Troutman, Samuel Riegel (teacher), Unknown Bahner, Unknown Smeltz, Paul Deppen, and Ralph Ferree.

Total 27 pupils.

CHAPTER 2

Forest School

Forest School (1865–1958). Photo taken in 1974, looking north. This school was built with wood at the edge of a forest on the Lesher Farm over the mountain from Urban. Some people called it the Lesher's School. Many Troutman family farms surrounded this school. Peter Trautman, the Mahantongo Valley pioneer, dwelled immediately west of this building. Norma Adams is the owner of the Peter Trautman Family dwelling site. George T. Troutman lived east of this school where Kieth Kembel's residence and farm is today. Photo courtesy of Jack Leitzel.

The Forest School was a one-room school known as School House #2. It was located on the road between Hebe and Urban. It was built in 1865 and utilized until 1958. A deed on file at the Northumberland County Court House refers to the acreage consisting of 39 square perches of land. At the time of purchase, the property was surrounded by many Troutman landowners, including Peter and May Troutman, Cornelius Troutman, and George T. Trautman. In later years, the school was referred to as Lesher's School, as a Lesher farm was nearby. Peter Trautman previously owned this farm.

On May 5, 1959, the deed recorded at the Sunbury Court House listed the transfer of the property from the school district of Jordan Township to the Forest Community Hall

Forest School. Photo taken in February of 2024, looking south. The original schoolhouse had many uses over the years. It served as a lodge hall, as evidenced by the lodge furniture which was seen in the building. The building is now known as the Hebe Community Center. An addition was added to the east end. Family reunions are held here and it is also a polling place for voters in Jordan Township.

Association. The school district of Jordan Township, Northumberland County, transferred ownership to the Hall Association in consideration for the sum of $550. This being the same premises which Peter Trautman and May, his wife, by their indenture bearing date the 21st day of May 1869.[1] Granted and surveyed under the school district.

By resolution passed on July 9, 1958, the said school district declared it to be the intention to vacate the Forest School, and the resolution passed on February 12, 1959, and the school district resolved to sell the Forest School at public sale. It was sold on March 14 at a public sale to the Forest Community Hall Association, Roscoe Troutman, Secretary.[2]

Clair Troutman recalls his attendance at Forest School. He was born in 1941 and attended first grade in 1947. He was transported by bus from his home to the school. Vern Leitzel of Hebe was the teacher. Clair attended Forest School through 1949, completing the third grade. He then attended Hebe school in grades four, five, and six. Jacob Hoffman was the teacher. He attended Dalmatia school for grades seven through eleven and graduated in 1959 with the first class to graduate from the new Mahanoy Joint High School.

Forest School Records

Steve Scott of SR 3013, Herndon, Pennsylvania, purchased a school record book on public sale. The hard-covered book is identified on the first page as *Teacher's Monthly Reports-Forest School, Number Two, Jordan Township District, Northumberland County, Pennsylvania*. Issued by the Department of

---

1 Recorded in the Office of the Recorder of Deeds in Deed Book 64, page 401.
2 Book 393, page 22.

Common Schools, June 1865, Harrisburg. Singerly and Myers, State Printers, 1865.

The second and third pages record the following describing the nineteen pupils: 10 males and 9 females. Report of Jno. A. Laudenschlager, Teacher of Forest School, No. Two, for the lunar month ending December 31, 1868. The ages of the children are recorded.

Male pupils: John Troutman, 8, George Troutman, 11, Adam Troutman, 12, Peter Kratzer, 18, Amos Kratzer, 16, Sam Troutman, 11, Isaac Troutman, 19, Jacob Lesher, 13, John Reigle, 8, Winebert Starr, 11. Female pupils: Amelia Bohner, 12, Mary Bohner 13, Amelia Troutman, 11, Esther Troutman, 14, Mary L. Troutman, 16, Phoebe Troutman, 9, Jane Troutman, 7, Sarah Zerbe, 9, Sarah Bush, 10.

Male pupil attendance as recorded: John and George Troutman attended 22 days with perfect attendance. The smallest attendance recorded was 4 days. Female pupil attendance was recorded: Mary L. Troutman, 16 days; Sarah Bush, 15 days; Esther Troutman, 14 days. The smallest attendance recorded was 7 days.

Books used and number of copies available: *Union ABC*, 2; *Sander's Primer*, 4; *Sander's Speller*, 6; *Sander's First Reader*, 1; *Sander's Second Reader*, 2; *Sander's Third Reader*, 1; *Sander's Fourth Reader*, 2; *Davis Written*, 4; *Brooks Mental*, 2.

Receipt, Received the 2nd day of Jan., 1869 . . . Thirty Dollars full salary, Jno. A. Laudenschlager, Teacher.

The Report of H.C. Drumheller, Teacher of Forest School, No. Two, for the lunar month ending December 31, 1872, Jordan District.

Thirty male pupils and sixteen female pupils were identified.

A roll call was called the first thing in the morning and afternoon. Attendance was

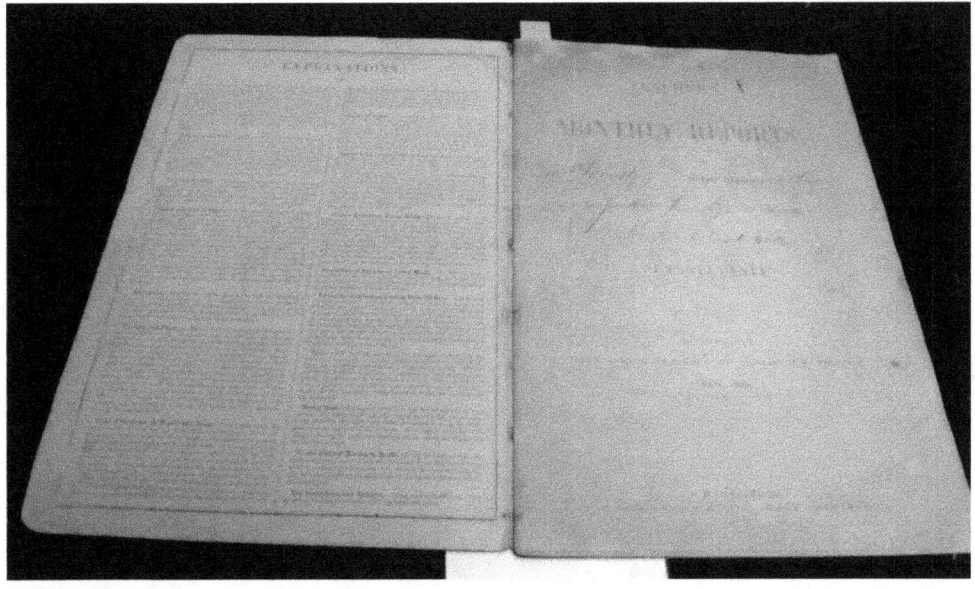

A Monthly Report.

recorded by using incomplete or complete crosses. Lateness in the morning was marked by a horizontal line. Lateness or absence in the afternoon was recorded by a vertical line, completing the cross. If the student was present for the morning and afternoon sessions, the space remained blank. An examination of this attendance record by the reader will note the large number of students absent all day, as recorded by the complete crosses.

Names and ages of male pupils: John A. Hoke, 9; Benjamin F. Hoke, 6; John A. Troutman, 6; Joel Masser, 8; Ferdinant Masser, 6; Henry Troutman, 10; Franklin Brocious, 6; John Deitrich 12; John Masser, 13; William Masser, 12; James Wagner 15; Ferdinant Wagner, 10; Lewis Kemble, 10; John H. Troutman, 10; John H. McKoy, 12; Elias Bush, 8; Joel Troutman, 12; Poisavel Kemble, 16; James D. Kratzer, 20; Peter Kratzer, 17; Franklin Troutman, 7; David Troutman, 9; John H. Rigel, 10; Henry Camp, 10; William Wagner, 17; V.B. Wiest, 16; Cossom Troutman, 10; Samuel Troutman, 16; George R. Troutman, 7; Franklin Bush, 14.

Names and ages of female pupils: Loretta F. Troutman, 8; Emma J. Schaffer, 10; Catherine E. Clark, 8; Catherine J. Kemble, 9; Anna J. Brocious, 8; Susanna Hoke, 12; Sarah F. Hoke, 15; Mary Masser, 10; Mary A. Wagner, 10; Christian Troutman, 12; Sivilla Schaffer, 15; Sarah Zerbe, 14; Sarah Bush, 8; Sarah A. Reigel, 9; Lydia Troutman, 8; Sarah E. Troutman, 15.

Sixty-four copies of books were available. The teacher was paid $30. The report was filed, examined and approved this 28th day of December, 1872. William A. Sheffer, Secretary.

Report of W. D. Baumgartner, Teacher of ____ School, ____ Township, ____ District.

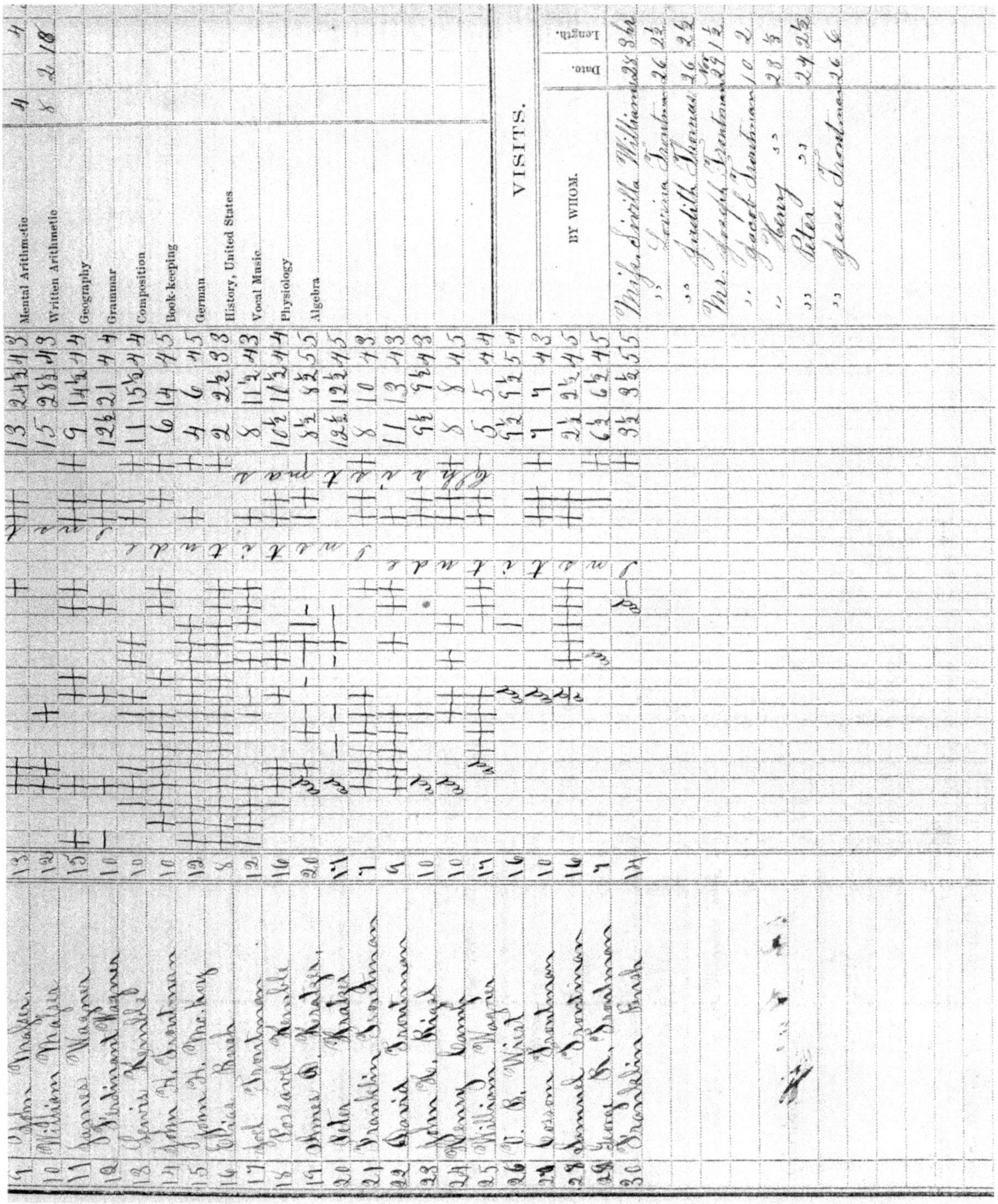

Mental Arithmetic
Written Arithmetic
Geography
Grammar
Composition
Book-keeping
German
History, United States
Vocal Music
Physiology
Algebra
VISITS.
BY WHOM.
Date.
Length.

Northumberland County.

No. 2, for the Fourth Month ending December 31, 1872.

NAMES OF Female PUPILS.	Age	ATTENDANCE. DAYS OF THE MONTH.	Total attendance in month.	Total attendance in term.	Progress.	Conduct.	BOOKS USED.	Number of each
				143			Sanders' Union Fifth Readers	5
1 Urella B. Bertram	8		12	24	5	5	" " Fourth "	3
2 Emma A. Schaffer	10		15	26	5	4	" " Third "	6
3 Katherine E. Clark	8		13	27	3	3	" " Second "	5
4 Catherine J. Kemble	8		4	12	3	5	Spellers	15
5 Anna J. Barrows	12		10	18	5	4	Pierces	10
6 Susanna Koke	15		10	15	5	5	Brookes Methods Arith.	1
7 Sarah E. Plohr	10		16	19	4	4	" Mental "	1
8 Mary Maginn	10		8	14	3	3	Robinson's Sequel to Arith.	2
9 Mary N. Wagner	12		12	22	5	4	" Rudiments "	4
10 Christiana Landsman	15		5	12	5	5	" Mental "	3
11 Cecelia Schaffer	14		12	13	4	5	Davis New & Old Wrtr.	2
12 Sarah O'Neil	8		6	6	4	4		
13 Anna Babb	9		6	9	5	5		
14 Sarah A. Bright	8		2	2	5	5		
15 Sophia Landsman	12							
16 Sarah L. Landsman								

No. of pupils without necessary books
" " days school open during month 18
" " " " during term till date 42

CERTIFICATE.

I certify that the foregoing Report of the number of scholars belonging to School since the first of June, attendance, books used, branches

Forest School / 11

Forest School, 1928.

Front row sitting (L to R): William Kimmel, Robert Kratzer, Ralph Kratzer, Paul Bohner, William Kratzer, Jay Bohner, Harry Kimmel, Francis Adams.

Second row (L to R): Harlen Lahr, Elwyn Boyer, Carl Schlegel, Raymond Kehler, Emery Maurer, Marlin Hepler, Raymond Strohecker, and Nevin Boyer.

Third row (L to R): Arlene Boyer, Mary Kratzer, Lena Maurer, Marion Lahr, Daisy Reed, Dorothy (or Miriam) Lahr, Violet Kratzer, Miriam Kratzer, and Grace Troutman.

Back row (L to R): Kathryn Lahr, Mildred Bohner, William "Cracker" Schlegel (teacher), Pauline Boyer, and Grace Kratzer.

Total 30 ppils.

Forest School, 1938.

Front row sitting (L to R): Robert Strohecker, Marvin Wiest, John Boyer, Paul Maurer, Clair Kimmel, Darvin Kahler, and Albert Strohecker.

Middle row (L to R): Romaine Mattern, Geraldine Kimmel, Esther Kahler, Mable Strohecker, Anna Kahler, Lucille Strohecker, Eleanor Troutman, Gladya Maurer, Violet Kahler, Kermit Bingaman, and Lawrence Strohecker.

Back row (L to R): Bernice Bingaman, Betty Troutman, Faye Strohecker, Hanna Weist, Eve Kimmel, William Schlegel (teacher), Vesta Wiest, Emma Wiest, Cleo Miller, Blanche Kimmel, and Doris Kimmel.

Total 28 pupils. Photo courtesy of Jack Leitzel of Hebe.

Third-grade class at Forest School, 1947.

Front row sitting (L to R): Lamar Leitzel, Richard Zeiders, Clair Troutman, Ray Williard, James Laudenslager, Dennis Boyer, Charles Witmar, Jack Adams, Paul Bingaman, Darvin Troutman, Dean Paul, Derl Boyer, and Melvin Bohner.

Second row (L to R): Janet Pelfer, Shirley Troutman, Arlene Boyer, Sandra Troutman, Veronica Coleman, Barbara Romberger, Darlene Kratzer, Louise Kahler, Phyllis Troutman, Fay Ferree, Dorene Hepler, and Shirley Boyer.

Third row (L to R): Irene Witmer, Romaine Schlegel, Doris Stohecker, Anna Strohecker, Joan Strohecker, Esther Paul, Marvin Paul, Maynard Kratzer, and Dennis Leitzel.

Back row (L to R): Donald Ferree, Roger Bohner, Mark Romberger, Mark Strohecker, David Bingaman, Melvin Adams, and teacher Warren Leitzel.

The "Upper Class" (7th and 8th grade) in Forest School, 1912–1913.

Left to right: John H. Bahner (teacher). Mary Leitzel, Edwin Troutman, Mabel Leitzel, Lawrence Leitzel, Carrie E. Bahner (my mother), Ray Troutman, Stella Knorr, and Hope Herr. Carrie (Bahner) Romberger made the identifications circa 1964.

Photo and narrative provided by John A. Romberger.

This typical one-room schoolhouse is still standing (in 2001). It still contains some of the original slate blackboards and also some of the original woodwork. The building is now used as a polling place for Jordan Township.

Beginning in about 1964, the Adam and Sarah Bahner Family Reunion has been held here on Memorial Day each year. Prior to then, that reunion was held in the picnic grove of the Stone Valley Church near Hickory Comers in the neighboring Lower Mahanoy Township.

CHAPTER 3

Grove School

Grove School, circa 1910.

William Troutman is the teacher. William is the father of Roscoe Troutman. This school stood across the road from Ray Kratzer's residence. A few foundation stones remain in the grass between the small stream and Bruce Troutman's Lane. This school was torn down after the Hebe school was built where James Troutman of Hebe, (Herndon, R.D.) now lives. Photo from Marion Troutman and Mrs. Guy (Blanch) Troutman.

Grove School was located south of the intersection of Klingerstown Road and Hebe Bypass Road.

A Recent Purchase

The Northumberland County Historical Society was recently able to purchase the 1897 copybook of Wesley Galen Trautman of Hebe. Son of Adam Lesher Trautman and Lavina Wolf Latsha, he first married Daisy W. Klinger. After her death, he married Fronie V. (Wiest) Stutzman. There were no children from either marriage. Through his mother's family, he was descended from Frans Latshow, a native of Switzerland who came to America on the sailing vessel *Mortonhouse*, which qualified at Philadelphia on August 24, 1728.[3]

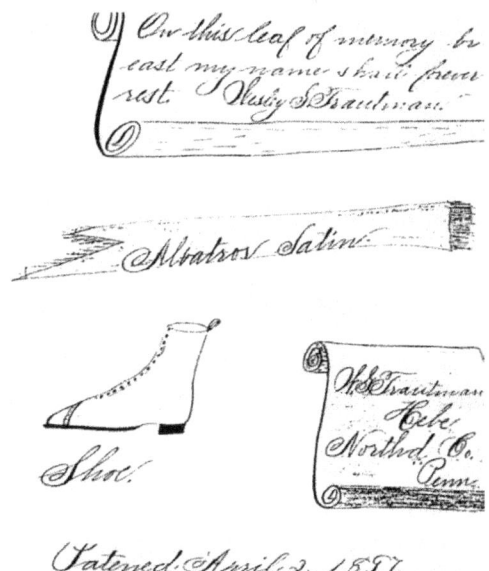

Scholars of Grove School No. 3.

1. Grandy G. Troutman
2. Clarena G. Troutman
3. Homer F. Bush
4. Harry F. Bush
5. Guerney V. Maurer
6. Samuel J. Maurer
7. Henry W. Engel
8. Wesley G. Troutman
9. John J. Peifer
10. Joseph C. Nether
11. Chas. W. Deppen
12. Daniel A. Deppen
13. Charles Maurer
14. Jacob M. Bohner
15. John A. Trautman
16. Ulissus S. Bohner
17. Francis Zahn
18. Chas Bohner
19. Allen S. Deppen
20. John H. Bohner

1. Ida S. E. Trautman
2. Maggie Engel
3. Nellie Troutman
4. Bertha Bohner
5. Blanche Bush
6. Bessie Bush
7. Birdie Bush
8. Macie Troutman
9. Fannie S. Deppen
10. Aldia C Enderson
11. Katie S. Merkel
12. Mary L Shoticker
13. Minnie Deppen
14. Minnie S. Shadel
15. Katie L. Deppen
16. Mandy Wiest
17. Carrie Wiest

---

3 From *The Trautman/Troutman Family History, Volume II*, by Steve E. Troutman.

CHAPTER 4

Hebe School

Hebe School (1918–1958). Photo taken in 1974. The Hebe School was built when the Grove School was abandoned and located in the village of Hebe.

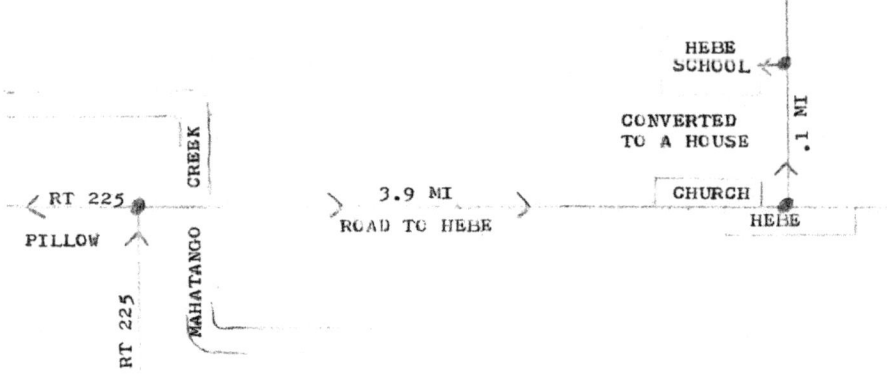

Hebe - Newport

Hebe—pronounced Heebee—is located in Jordan Township, a few miles east of Urban. It was known originally as "Newport." When a request for a post office was submitted to the postal department, the postal authorities replied that there was already a post office by the name of Newport in Juniata County, now zip code 17974. The postal department submitted the name of Hebe, which was accepted. Who was Hebe? Hebe was a deity in mythology. She was a daughter of Juno; she was the goddess of youth and Jupiter's cupbearer but was banished from heaven on account of an unlucky fall. An inland town with a prefix or suffix containing the word "port" would be located along a body of water, for example, Port Trevorton—Pennsylvania canal. Walnutport—Lehigh canal. Some people thought the name was of Indian origin, while most of them didn't know.

John E. Deppen operated a farm and worked as a carpenter for the Philadelphia & Reading Railroad. He built a hotel in Hebe and was appointed as postmaster

Hebe School, 1938.

Front row sitting (L to R): Ray Kratzer, Lawrence Strohecker, Lester Leitzel, Donald Long, Robert Smeltz, William Bohner, George Strohecker, Dean Bohner, Marvin Leitzel, Richard Strohecker, Lee Straub, and Stewart Leitzel.

Second row (L to R): Jack Leitzel, Russell Weller, Ruth Smeltz, Leanore Williams, Ester Strohecker, Annabel Shaffer, Rozella Erdman, Iva Straub, Arlene Leitzel, Helen Laudenslager, Ester Fegley, Martha Adams, Colleen Weller, Loraine Leitzel, and Jay Long.

Third half row (L to R): Marion Straub, Grace Leitzel, Lila Bohner, Ethel Leitzel, Betty Fegley, and Marion Schlegel.

Back row (L to R): Nelson Straub, Paul Hoffman, Ruby Leitzel, Annabel Hoffman, Violet Reed, Emory Leitzel (teacher), Mildred Shaffer, Bertha Strohecker, Ray Shaffer, Ralph Bohner, William Strohecker, and Ned Peifer.

Total 44 pupils.

during the Benjamin Harrison administration. He served in that capacity for 12 years. He then accepted an appointment as turnkey at the county prison in Sunbury. He died on October 20, 1902. Charles Deppen succeeded him and I believe that he was the last postmaster when the office was discontinued. He transferred the post office from the hotel building to his home on the same side of the street.

The Hebe School House has been converted into a lovely residence. Photo taken February 3, 2024.

The school was located north of David's Church near the center of Hebe.

The Hebe School was built after the removal of the Grove School. Grove School was located east of Hebe on the intersection of Klingerstown Road and Hebe Bypass Road.

Hebe School, 1947.

Front row sitting (L to R): Mark Peifer, Alfred Troutman, Paul Troutman, Ted Troutman, Billy Leitzel, Milan Kratzer, and Russell Bohner. Second row (L to R): Roy Romberger, Mabel Boyer, Romaine Klinger, Jean Hoffman, Mary Witmer, Arlene Klinger, Shirley Adams, and Betty Kimmel. Third row (L to R): William Bohner Jr., Alma Strohecker, Marlene Leitzel, Anna Witmer, Janet Laudenslager, Joan Troutman, Carol Leitzel, and Ronald Boyer. Back row (L to R): Rita Hepler, Leona Adams, William "Cracker" Schlegel (teacher), and Orpha Troutman.

Total 27 pupils. Photo courtesy of Dennis Boyer Photo Collection.

Old-Time School Teachers in the Hebe Area

Elwyn Boyer Photo Collection. This picture was taken between 1907 and 1915 because Ulysses Bohner died in February 1915 when he was 28. These men are Hebe area schoolteachers.
Front row sitting (L to R): Grant Troutman, William L. Troutman, John Bohner, and Ulysses Bohner.

Back row standing (L to R): William Troutman, Naldy Leitzel, Earl Troutman, and Jacob Hoffman.

Jacob taught at the Hebe School until the 1950s. William L. Troutman taught in a school east of Hebe called Nobel School.

CHAPTER 5

Nobel (Rothermel's) School

John Romberger Recalls his Early School Days at the Nobel (Rothermel's) School Jordan Township, Northumberland County, Pennsylvania

Several years ago, the Gratz Historical Society held a summertime meeting at the Kessler's one-room schoolhouse in the village of Erdman. John A. Romberger was the speaker on the topic of one-room schools. John attended Nobel School in Jordan Township, about one mile west of Klingerstown. He lived next door to this school in a house built by Civil War veteran William Rothermel. This was locally known as Rothermel's School on Rothermel's Run. John's presentation included a few memorable occurrences from his days at this one-room school.

One day, while class was in session at Nobel School, there was an urgent knock on the door. Andy Schwalm, a farmer near the school, on the east toward Klingerstown, was calling loudly in Pennsylvania German dialect, "*Kumme raus. Kumme raus. Sis ebbes zu sehna.*" (Come out. Come out. There is something to see.) Andy was wearing his barn coat and boots as he had come running straight from his barn chores. He pointed toward the heavens, where a large, motorized blimp was slowly making its way westward across the sky. The children exited the school. They saw something they had never seen before. As I recall John telling the story, he later learned that this was the Navy airship *Macon*. The *Macon* met its end in 1935 when it plunged into the Pacific Ocean. It was the last of the giant rigid constructed airships owned by the Navy. It was 785 feet long, being built in 1933.

Another event that John Romberger recalled was the occasion when the farmer's water pipe froze. Nobel School was built near Rothermel's Run. This stream crossed under the highway on the west side of the school. A pasture for the Schwalm's dairy cows was located north of the school. The watering trough was located along the main road. Sometimes, cattle from the Schwalm's barn were led up the road to the trough to drink. The summer had been dry, and water was scarce. To make things worse, the fall continued to be dry. The small amount of water in Rothermel's Run was ponded up to fill a pipe, which led to the road-side water trough. Cold nights with temperatures below freezing froze the slow-flowing water in the fill pipe. Water was needed for the livestock. It was decided to wrap the iron pipe with burlap bags. Coal oil was poured on the burlap, and it was lit on fire. The long line of flames burned brightly and furiously. The hot metal pipe thawed open, water flowed, and the cows could drink once more at the trough.

John recalled the dirt road in front of the school. It was covered with macadam while school was in session. The school children were allowed to watch the road construction as crushed stone and tar were put in place and rolled to form a paved road surface. The boys re-enacted this road building at recess in the sandy soil behind the school. They built their own roads.

Gail Romberger Nonnecke of Roland, Iowa, provided the following picture showing the Nobel School. Gail wrote, "The picture is from my dad, Roland Romberger. He took it in 1936 with a camera his father, Stanley, had given him when Roland was 12 or 13 years old. Roland said Allen S. Rothermel would hook a large white pine log to his horse to clear a pathway for the students to walk to school."

Dr. John A. Romberger made some comments about Roland's picture below. John grew up at the house seen in the picture of Nobel's school.:

Dear Steve, thank you most sincerely for the photographic print of the old homestead. This picture has many clues that allow approximate dating. 1. The electric line had already been put in but there is no transformer for this house. 2. The road had been already regraded. 3. The old smokehouse is still standing. 4. The old garden fence is still there. 5. The hillside in the foreground has not been planted to trees. 6. The pig pens have not yet been reconstructed. 7. The house has not yet been painted white. All in all, I would say that the picture was taken in very late 1936 or early 1937. We

Earl and Marion (Romberger) Troutman Residence April 1943 to October 1962. Photo by Roland Romberger, age 12 or 13, in 1936. Allen Rothermel pulled a white pine log with his team of black horses to clear a pathway for students to walk to school. Steve, Glenn and Ruby grew up on this farm.

moved back from the Klingerstown Mill in April of 1936. In the spring of 1939, we began a series of changes and improvements which continued through 1944. I went away to the Army in early 1945. My parents sold the place to your grandfather in October of 1945 and moved to Hershey.

Teacher Vern Leitzel was the instructor for all subjects, one of which was science. There was a solar eclipse of the sun forecast in the newspaper by astronomers. The students were told they could view the eclipse by looking through smoked glass. Instructions were given as to how to prepare smoked glass. Those who could do this should bring their glass to school on the day of the eclipse. John's father, Ralph Romberger, was an early photographer. He had dark glass from developing photographs. He gave this glass to his son John, to use to view the eclipse. The John Rothermel boys and girls who lived further up Rothermel's Run had a different idea. There was an abandoned automobile on the farm. Or perhaps it was an old truck. The boy removed the windshield, built a fire, and successfully smoked the glass. The Rothermel children showed up at school with the largest piece of smoked glass! It was so big that they could actually sit behind the windshield as they viewed the eclipse.

Some additional information that I can add about the Nobel School concerns my mother. Some of the children in the school could not speak English when they arrived for first grade. My mother, Marion

Nobel School in the late afternoon sun, early 1980s. Rothermel Run eventually undermined the southwest corner of the foundation. By this time, the roof deterioration was becoming advanced, and then eventually collapsed. Presently, the foundation stones can still be found next to the run.

Romberger, lived ¼ mile east of the school. She spoke the Pennsylvania German dialect at home with her parents and older brothers. This was the language used by everyone in the area. Marion soon learned to speak English at the Nobel School, where the English vocabulary was much preferred. Despite the fact that she knew no English when she entered school, she became one of the best spellers. Ray Davis and my mother were often in spelling bees. Ray told me he would have often been in the first place if Marion wouldn't have been in the contest. Ray settled for the second-best speller. Later in her life, Marion traveled to Germany to research her Romberger family roots. The ancestral German dialect allowed her to communicate very well with the people of Bavaria and Austria. Here, she made many Romberger acquaintances. As a youth, my father, Earl, learned to speak both languages at home. He could speak English when he went to school and Pennsylvania Dutch home on the farm and at work.

A new Amish one-room school is being built in 2015 near where I live in Rough and Ready. The David Ray Stoltzfus family is the first Amish family to live in what I term to be Rough and Ready. The Amish folks have arrived in the valley with their children. They as well will learn to speak English in the new one-room school.

Nobel School, located between Hebe and Klingerstown. Your photographer, Steve E. Troutman, lived next to this one-room schoolhouse as a boy. His parents, Earl G. Troutman and. Marion A. Romberger, attended here through elementary grades. Michael and Valerie Troutman pose, 1983.

The following story was related to Steve E. Troutman by John D. Troutman, the son of Victor Troutman, who attended "Pig Town" school. It seems William Troutman was the schoolmaster at this school for many years. In his later years, he allowed the children to be quite noisy so that there was little difference between school time and recess time. During William's last years as a teacher, some of the local farm boys appeared to have had the upper hand with the teacher, as when Manassis Rothemal and Al Williard drilled a hole through the floor beside their desks in order to spit tobacco juice during school hours!

Nobel School, 1938.

Front row sitting (L to R): Bryant Rothermel, Bruce Troutman, Earl Troutman, Bobby Hoffman, and Glenn Leitzel.

Middle row (L to R): Rosie Boyer, Roxie Leitzel, Anna Rothermel, Lee Romberger, Shirley Rothermel, Marion Romberger, Jean Rothermel, and Bryant Troutman.

Back row (L to R): Miriam Shadel, Roxie Rothermel, Racheal Deitz, Warren Leitzel (Teacher), John Romberger, Ray Leitzel, and Kenneth Boyor.

Total 19 pupils.

Rothermel's School as it appeared in 1923. (This is the little, red, one-room schoolhouse attended by my paternal grandmother, my father, my sister Marie, and myself.)

Rothermel School Memories
by John A. Romberger

Rothermel's school, also known as "Nobel" school, was one of seven built in Jordan Township of Northumberland County, Pennsylvania. All were built in 1864 or 1865, but the order of their construction or completion is not known. This schoolhouse was located on a small lot just across (to the east) Rothermel's Run from the "Old Billie Rothermel" homestead, which is where Marie and I grew up, though we were not born there. This old Rothermel house, now considerably enlarged, is (in 2001) occupied by Joseph Michetti and family.

The date "1922" painted on the front gable end above the diamond window refers to the date of the painting. The base color was barn red, and the trim was white. The print from which I made this enlargement is dated "December 1923." It was given to me by Mark Wiest, whose mother, Dora Troutman Wiest, had attended this school when she was young. The photographer cannot be identified.

When I began attending school here in the fall of 1931, the appearance of the building was much as shown here, except that an entrance shelter had been added around the front door. The teacher that year was Warren G. Leitzel.

The building was used without further alteration during the 1930s and early 1940s, though some minor exterior repairs were made. It stood vacant for some years in the late 1940s and early 1950s. Finally, the roof collapsed. The building was demolished, probably in about 1960, to make way for a large pond which now occupies part of the site.

Rothermel's School Pupils in February of 1914. (The tall boy in the back row is Ralph T. Romberger.)

The picture was taken inside the school building shown in the previous picture in this collection. The pupils, beginning with the back row from the left, are Ruth Rothermel (Snyder), Lizzie Schwalm (Rebuck), Florence Mae Schwalm (Rothermel), Hannah Rothermel (Leitzel), Norman Rothermel, Clara Willard (Rudisill), Katie Schwalm (who died young), Stella Schlegel (Wiest), Ralph T. Romberger, Mervin Leitzel, Robert Rothermel, Harvey Schadel, Ida Rothermel (teacher, later Mrs. Jay Phillips). Front row from left: Tren Wiest, Mary Williard (Morgan), Fred Williams, Mabel Rothermel (Williard), Ethel Rothermel (Coleman), Charles Rothermel Herb, Minnie Rothermel (Bixler), Mabel Schwalm (who was a school visitor that day), Raymond Williams, Nathan Schwalm, Charles Williard, Howard Willard, Melvin Wiest, and John Rothermel. Names in parentheses are married names.

All the Schwalm children in the picture were siblings. Norman, Ida, Mabel (?), Ethel, Minnie. and John Rothermel were siblings (the children of Lazarus Rothermel). Fred and Raymond Williams were brothers.

All of these children lived within walking distance of the school. Only rarely did parents bring or pick up their children, and in 1914, few families had cars.

Identifications were made with the help of Daniel Schwalm, who had another copy of the picture with identifications made by his parents, Nathan and Minnie Schwalm, many years ago.

Note the antique wallpaper above the blackboards. Some of this paper was still in place when I was a pupil there. The desks and slate blackboards were also the same.

One Room School House Memories Preserved by Wiseman Print

by Danelle Carvell

HERNDON – Anyone who attended a one-room schoolhouse knows how different life was then compared to today. Now those memories have been preserved by artist Deanna Wiseman in her limited-edition print *Dinner Time Ball Game*.

Wiseman's print depicts a spring day with students playing baseball in front of the Nobel schoolhouse. Some children sit in the grass, watching the game and eating their lunches while a 1936 Ford approaches on a dirt road.

Roland Romberger attended first through eighth grades at the Nobel School, which was built in Jordan Township near Klingerstown in 1865. Originally named the Rothermel School because of the many Rothermel families in the area, the Nobel School was a "typical little red" schoolhouse that measured thirty by thirty feet.

Physically, all that remains of the school today is a stone foundation and a rusted pot-bellied stove lying on its side. The school closed in 1958, but memories of the Nobel School are still vivid among some of the local people who attended. Bryant Troutman remembers many details about the days of the one-room schoolhouse, right down to what students packed in their lunches.

"We brought butter and salt along in our dinner buckets," said Troutman. The pot-bellied stove had a "jacket" covering. "It was an excellent potato backer, which many children used," he said. The potatoes were placed between the stove and the jacket.

John Romberger, who also attended the Nobel School, lived nearby and walked home for lunch. But he remembers the potatoes. "By 11:00, the smell of baking potatoes pervaded the room," he said. And even today when Romberger smells baked potatoes, he thinks of the school.

John's mother, Carrie Romberger, would set the stove each morning when the weather was cold. Then when John was in seventh and eighth grade, his teacher paid him twenty-five cents a week to open the school and fire the stove. Another nearby neighbor, Stanley Romberger, supplied drinking water, which was carried in buckets to fill a five-gallon porcelain water fountain. Some students brought milk, which they kept cool in the stream that ran behind the schoolhouse.

Along with baked potatoes, some other "dinner bucket" favorites were apple butter bread, snitz pie, egg sandwiches, smoked sausage, and friend rabbit and squirrel. Hunting was a popular way to provide food.

According to Troutman, one of his teachers, Warren Leitzel, brought his shotgun to school during small game season. "He would hunt during the dinner house and then showed us what he brought back," he said. One of the boys in the class was a trapper and sometimes he came to school smelling like a skunk. When asked if the smell was a distraction, Troutman laughed and said, "It was no big deal. We all lived in the country. That happens."

About twenty students at a time attended the Nobel School, according to old photographs and Troutman's recollection. He remembers that the school day ran from 8 AM to 4 PM and started with the reading of scripture, prayer, and the pledge of allegiance. The girls sat on one side of the room, and the boys on the other.

Along with their lessons, students memorized poems and recited them. "Paul Revere's Ride" and "Woodman Spare That Tree" are two of many poems Troutman recalls having to memorize. Singing was also a part of the school day, especially on Friday, when everyone sang along to songs like "The Little Brown Church" and "Row, Row, Row Your Boat." At the close of school each Friday, a student volunteered to wash the chalkboard and clap the erasers.

The school year began September 1st and continued through April. "We didn't have half days or in-service days, and we didn't get a week off for Christmas," Troutman said. The only half day he remembers occurred on Thanksgiving, and if Christmas fell on a weekday, students got the whole day off. Sometimes, the older boys were excused early to help with the harvest or other farm work.

Troutman also recalls the school inside and most of the standard equipment used by both the teachers and the students. A large clock and pictures of Washington and Lincoln hung on the wall. Usually, a piano or organ occupied the room as well as coal oil lamps, a broom, and a coal bucket for fueling the pot-bellied stove. A hand-held bread toaster was used to toast bread over the stove. Also used was a large dictionary, a Bible, an American flag, and a hand-held bell, which the teacher rang at noon break and in the morning after recess to call the students inside.

John Romberger remembers sharing a double desk with Troutman's brother, Earl, in seventh and eighth grades. "All the desks were double width and built for two people," he said. "The desktops weren't hinged, but there was a shelf underneath to put books and pencils."

Graphite pencils and paper tablets were used when Romberger attended the Nobel School in the 1930s, but he said his parents also attended the school in the early 1900s and they used slate boards and slate pencils. "The desks had holes for ink bottles, and we did sometimes use liquid ink," said Romberger. "But kids had accidents with ink and it would freeze on the weekends unless they kept a fire in the stove. By the time I was in eighth grade, ink was no longer encouraged."

Dogs often followed students as they walked to the schoolhouse. "They stayed outside and played with the children at recess and dinner," Troutman said. To preserve that memory, Wiseman's print, of course, includes a dog.

During recess, the children entertained themselves with games like Fox in the Morning, Barley Over, and Dog and Deer. They also floated small boats in the stream. In the winter, they made igloos and went sleigh riding.

Hide and Seek and Tag were the most popular games. Shootball was another favorite according to John Romberger. It was played like baseball, except the ball was made of soft rubber. "We tried to hit the runner with the ball instead of throwing to a base," he explained.

Students were interactive inside the school as well. "The older students helped the younger ones," said Troutman. Warren Leitzel and Jacob "Jeck" Hoffman were his teachers while attending the Nobel School. "Both excellent teachers," he said. "They taught one on one. If someone didn't understand, they went to that student and explained it until he did." But sometimes the students played practical jokes that didn't go over well with the teacher.

During his first year at the school, Troutman had a seat in back, near the door. On Faasnacht Day, also known as Shrove Tuesday, the older boys tied the door shut to keep the teacher out. "It was a tradition years ago," he said. Mr. Leitzel shook the door so violently that the chain fell off and he came into the school swinging a broom. "He was angry," said Troutman. "My buddy and I climbed under the seat in fright."

With all the fun and games that went on at the Nobel School, former students said they got a good education. "The quality of instruction was good," said John Romberger. Because the younger students sat up front, they could hear the upper classes reciting their lessons over and over. "By the time we got to seventh and eighth grades, we heard the material repeated several times," he said.

Concerning education, Troutman says there is much to learn in the Holy Scriptures: Proverbs 1:5 tells us: "A wise man will hear and will increase learning; and a man of understanding shall attain unto wise council." Looking back on those days at the Nobel schoolhouse, he recalls an educational environment quite different from today. "Anybody who didn't get to a one-room schoolhouse really missed out on an experience," he said. For him, it was an experience worth preserving.

Bryant Troutman may be seen on page 27 in the 1938 Nobel School group photo.

CHAPTER 6

Linden School

Linden School, 1911.

Linden School was one of the original schools in Jordan Township. It was closed in 1917. Deed entered in Northumberland County Courthouse: Date November 2, 1872. Peter Troutman and wife to the Jordan Township School District. Today, this roadside location is on the property of Judy and Carl Mace, who reside between Urban and Klingerstown in the Hooflander Valley.[4]

A side note: As a boy growing up in the area, the author often heard the name for this part of Hoofland called "the Peter's Patch." No doubt, this name originates with the landowner, Peter Troutman.

---
4 Photo contributed by Shirley Silvick, October 25, 2006.

CHAPTER 7

Urban School

Urban School (1866–1958). Photo taken in 1974. The Urban School was built on a hill in the post-village and could be seen from all sides.

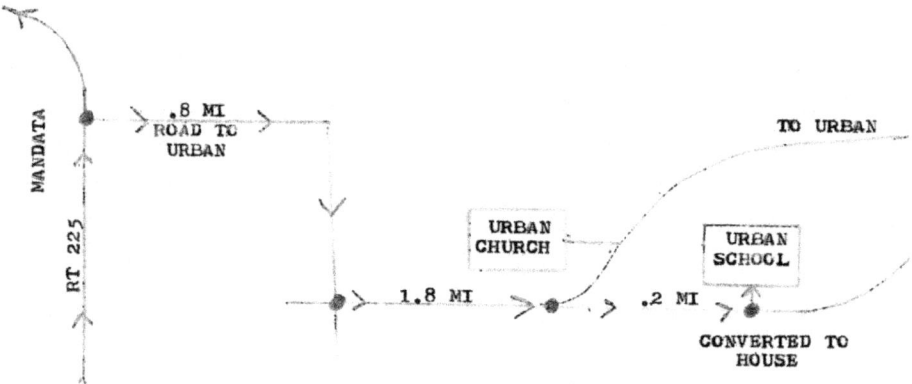

34 / One-Room Schoolhouses of the Mahantongo Valley

Urban is in the northern part of Jordan Township. An early settler by the name of Daniel Swartz built the first building and hotel. Urban became a post village when a post office was established, the name given by the postal department. Daisy Snyder was a postmaster at Urban and the old building where the post office was located was also a general country store; it was destroyed by fire about ten years ago. When the post office was discontinued about 1908 or thereabouts, rural free delivery service emanated from the Pillow (Uniontown) post office in Dauphin County. Mail service to Jordan Township is furnished from the Herndon post office.

Urban was a horse trading center many years ago, and the old horse barn near the hotel is still standing.

Daniel Swartz and George Shartel had tanneries in the township in the early days. Aaron Schaeffer conducted the hotel in Jordan Township.

William Burkey, age 92, stopped by the Lewisburg Farm Market. He had a Golden Nugget pie pumpkin for Steve at the Troutman Brother's Meats stand. William's agricultural roots are deep in the Mahantongo Valley. He presently grows produce at his home in Shamokin Dam. The produce is of top quality and easily sold when market ready.

William was always proud of his Pennsylvania Dutch heritage and enjoys speaking the dialect. William was raised in Urban where he attended the one room school located on the hill top above town. Jacob Hoffman and William Schlegel were some of his first teachers. William Burky and Boyd Bordner were seated in the front of the room at a double seat school desk. William asked Boyd about a word written in the school book and leaned over to him to talk. The teacher was determined to keep order in the class. He got a long leather strap used as a horse trace. He said, "*My leder gail stang swichis neigelegt,*" (I place this leather horse trace between you), over the desk top and seats. "*Des ist my hund,*" (This is my dog), "and *wan dir eich net beheft,*" (and if you don't behave) "*den dut ah eich bise,*" (then it will bite you).

The teacher had the attention of the whole class. However, sometime later, the older boys managed to get the leather horse trace and cut it up and burn it in the school stove.

Urban School, 1937.

Front row sitting (L to R): Harry Bordner, William Shaffer, Fred Kiehl Jr., Alfred Schlegel, Robert Kissinger, Boyd Bordner, Thomas Bordner, George Baumert Jr., and Paul Bordner.

Middle row (L to R): William Burkey, Bruce Kiehl, Arthur Henning, Raymond Leffler, Margaret Shaffer, Rosie Snyder, Pauline Snyder, Anna Mae Shaffer, Hilda Houser, and Jean Kiehl.

Back row (L to R): Etherline Leffler, Carol Warner, Elwood Snyder, Melva Krissinger, William Schlegel (teacher), Shirley Kiehl, Ruth Schaffner, Eleanor Snyder, Marie Schaffner, and Margaret Leffler.

Total 28 pupils.

School House #58, Horton Photo, Urban, Pennsylvania. Urban School was rebuilt in 1901.

This postcard photo by an itinerant photographer named Horton was bought on eBay. Attempts to identify the location have been made. Early maps of the gap in Urban show a school located north of the gap. This building is not the Linden School, which was located in Hoofland Valley. The doorway, the attic window, and the entryway steps are different from the 1911 Linden School picture. Above the attic window there is identification written, which appears to be "JN No.6, Rebuilt 1901."

CHAPTER 8

Dubendorf (Gap) School

Dubendorf School (1865–1958). Picture taken in 1974. Courtesy of Jack Lietzel of Hebe. This wooden one-roomer was located in a gap west of Urban; some people called it the Gap School.

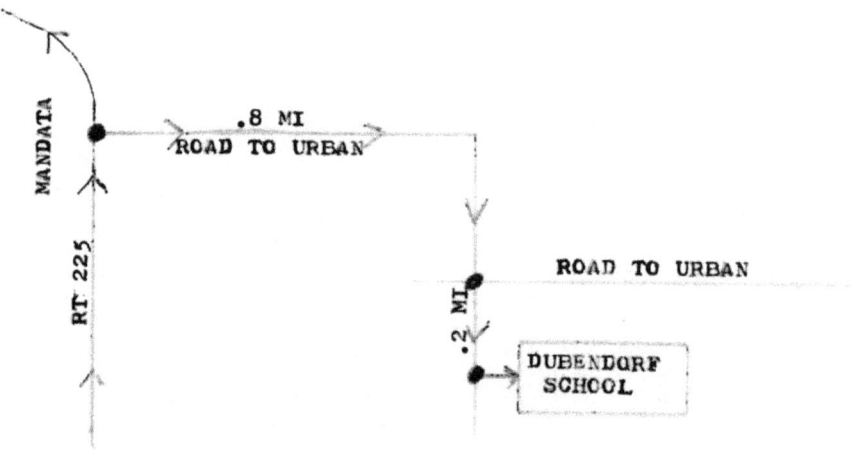

38 / One-Room Schoolhouses of the Mahantongo Valley

Dubendorf (Gap) School.

First row sitting (L to R): John Miller, Mark Yerger, Homer Yerger, Darvin Schlegel, Adam Lahr, Allen Ramer, Robert Went, and Howard Engle.

Middle row (L to R): Grant Heintzelman, Shirley Noecker, Dorthy Ramer, Yvonne Troxel, Dorothy Brown, Loretta Wolf, Marlene Byerly, Janet Wolf, Goldie Rebuck, and Mary Ramer.

Back row (L to R): Mae Heintzelman, Francis Adams, Cathrine Yerger, Ida Lahr, Geraldine Reitze (teacher), Margaret Snyder, Pauline Yerger, Eveline Ramer, and Shirley Grimm.

Total 27 pupils. Courtesy of Jack Leitzel of Hebe.

Mandata

Mandata is situated in the valley of Fiddler's Run and on the main road from Herndon to Pillow renamed Uniontown. It is now along Route 225 between Shamokin and Harrisburg.

The lines of Jordan, Lower Mahanoy and Jackson Townships converge at this point, and the village is located in three townships. The post office and general store were located in Jordan Township. Noah Klock, proprietor of the general store, was the first postmaster when the office was established. J. W. Seals operated a tannery in the village but it was located in Jackson Township. John Wirt built a grist mill in Jordan Township in 1838. The former Bull Run Tavern was located in Jackson Township and was operated by Daniel Lahr during the building of the Northern Central Railway.

A Pennsylvania State highway marker, made of cast iron, stands along Route 225, near the center of the village. It states "Mandata. Named for an Indian girl, who lived where the town is now located. Founded in 1880."

Mandata is known for its immense poultry processing plant, where it is said that 5,000 live poultry are processed daily under government inspection. Years ago, cast-off chicken parts such as feet, heads, and bones were frozen and exported to Asia to be used as food.

CHAPTER 9

Troutman School

Troutman School in Dauphin County. The Troutman School was vacated in the early 1900s and demolished in the early 1950s.

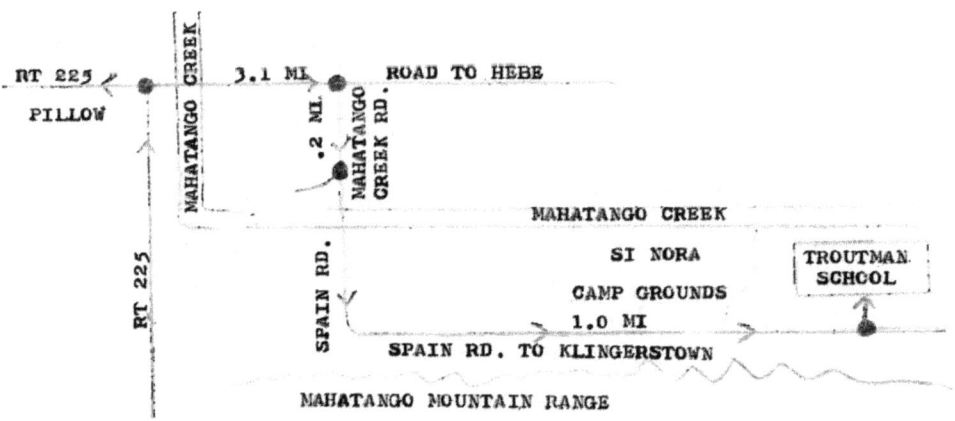

CHAPTER 10

Paul's School

Upper Mahanoy Township, Northumberland County, Pennsylvania

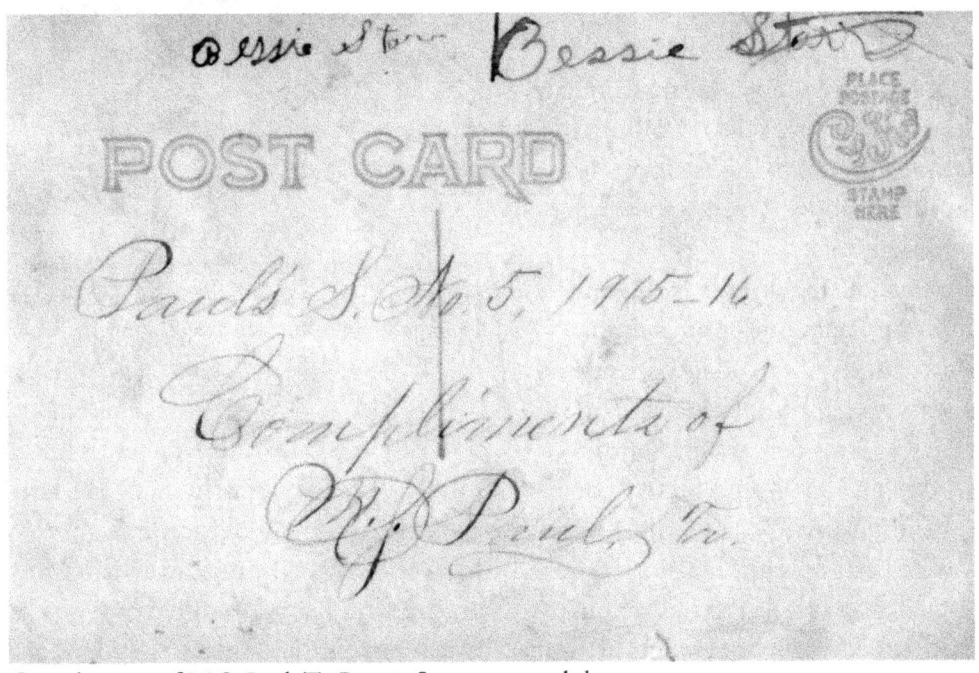

Compliments of M.S. Paul, Tr. Besssie Starr autograph.[1]

This postcard picture of "Paul's Academy" is courtesy of Mary Straub, of Hoffman Road, Upper Mahantongo Twp., Schuylkill County, PA. The name "Bessie Starr" is written on the back of the postcard. Bessie Starr is the daughter of John and Harriet Rebuck Starr and the sister of Mary Jane Starr Hoffman. Mary Jane is the wife of Harvey Clair Hoffman, who was a well-known mechanic and blacksmith in the Klingerstown area. Mary Straub, the granddaughter of Mary Jane and Harvey Clair Hoffman, provided the Paul School postal card information in September of 2024. The reverse of the card states, as addressed by the teacher, "Paul's S. #5, 1915–16. Compliments of M.S. Paul, Tr."

---

1 Bessie Starr lived at the Starr residence identified on the 1875 Map, one mile east of the school. This Starr residence is presently the Jessie Knorr Farm.

The photo postcard was given to Bessie by her teacher, Milton S. Paul. He lived locally on what is now Corner's Road. Milton lived on an old Knorr homestead, where Beatrice Paul was the last to occupy the dwelling. The house still stands in a pasture on the Ken Smith farm, which is on the north side of the hill adjoining Benigna's Winery.

The scene is a group photo of the teacher and 24 students. It must have been a chilly day when the photographer visited the school. Every boy and girl is wearing a substantial coat, and the girls all have head coverings of hats and scarves. Some boys are holding hats, and the teacher is holding his hat by his side. The schoolhouse looks like a typical German wooden-sided one-roomer with wooden shutters.

This is a rare photograph. It is the only known photo of Paul's one-room school, locally known as "Paul's Academy." Pauls' Academy was located on Old State Road. Khristyn Maurer's residence is presently located on this site, 1994 Old State Road, Dornsife, Pennsylvania. Willard and Joyce (Jones) Kahler built this house using some of the recycled wood from the old school. Willard dismantled the school when he built a home for himself. Willard attended this school as a young boy.

Willard grew up on the nearby Norman Kahler farm. Norman and Mildred Kahler had a large family. The Norman Kahler farm was earlier owned by David Paul and then by his son, Charles Paul. Norman and Mildred Kahler purchased the farm from Charles Paul during the Depression years. David Paul provided the plot of land for the schoolhouse.

Milton S. Paul may have been a school teacher all of his life. He also taught at the Delp School on Old State Road, about two miles west of Paul's School. The Delp School is a former dwelling of the late Charles Brown.

Willard recalled his teacher, John Clark. John Clark was a strong man. He often walked to school barefoot, even in the winter. John lived several miles away from the school on the farm lately occupied by Lee Clark, between Greenbriar and Leck Kill. Willard said he once climbed a tree at the schoolhouse to get away from Mr. Clark, the teacher, who wanted to discipline his student.

The 1875 Map of Mahanoy Twp., Northumberland County, Pennsylvania, shows the neighboring residents. D. Paul is shown as living on the farm where the schoolhouse was built. Other neighboring residents are identified on the 1875 map as Starr, Sheffer, Fetter, Kime, Beisel, Fetterolf, Hane, Berghouse,

Knorr, Ressler, Heim, and Smith. Although the students are not named on the picture, they must be from the above-named families.

Lamar Mattern, who has lived nearby all his life, recalls Norman Kahler using the school as a granary after it was abandoned. The blackboard was on the north side, and a vestibule provided the entrance. Lamar also stated that the property adjoining the school on the south is locally known as Paul's Patch. This area includes the farmland on the south side of Knorr Hollow Road and the woodland that adjoins Lamar's home.

The 1858 Map of Mahanoy Twp., Northumberland County, Pennsylvania, shows a school at this location identified as E and R School. This refers to the Evangelical and Reformed Church, which was associated with this site of early education prior to the establishment of public schools.

Paul's School #5, 1915–16. Mahanoy Township, Northumberland County, Pennsylvania, Mahantongo Valley.

CHAPTER 11

Stein's School

Stein's School, circa 1916.

Front row sitting (L to R): LeRoy Reed, Herlan Deitz, Spurgeon Minnich, Clair Reed, Floyd Maurer, Helen Minnich (Weaver), Katie Ramberger (Klinger), and Bessie Schadel (Bowman).

Back row standing (L to R): Carrie Shade, Flossie Reed (Reiner), Carrie Oxenrider (Smith), Florence Deitz (Geist), Carrie Snyder, (?), Pearl Deitz (Kieffer), Homer Snyder, Earl Oxenrider, and Walter Davis (teacher).

Total 17 pupils.

Stein's School still stands in a deteriorated condition. The school is located south of the Salem Church in Rough and Ready, on Valley Road, along the Little Mahantongo Creek.

Steins School, November 6, 1924.

Front row (L to R): Guy Knorr, Franklin Sherry, William Wolfgang, John Snyder, and William Bressler.

Second row (L to R): Willard Deitz, Darvin Feger, Clifford Maurer, Elwood Rothermel, Marlin Snyder, Marlin Deitz, Raymond Erdman, and Whalen Minnich.

Third row (L to R): Whalen Snyder, Mazie Feger, Lila Reed, Earl Minnich, Dorothy Ramberger (sister to Laura Ramberger), Dorothy Rothermel, Lillian Shadel, and Violet Reed.

Fourth row (L to R): Marlin Maurer, Elda Wolfgang, Irene Reed, Laura Ramberger (my grandma), Gertie Erdman, Myrtle Minnich, Helen Rothermel, and Mazie Shadel.

Back row (L to R): Clarence Fetterolf (teacher), Gertie Wolfgang, Alice Snyder, Evelyn Fetter, Lucille Snyder, Mae Haas, Iva Wolfgang, Twins Edna and Jennie Rothermel.

Total 38 pupils. Photo provided by Jeanne Adams. Student names were recalled by her grandmother, Laura Ramberger Klinger.

CHAPTER 12

Fetterolf School

Fetterolf School, 1930.

Front row sitting (L to R): Lawrence Maurer, Eugene Erdman, Harold Maurer (Lawrence's brother), Paul Martin, and Bernard Adams (brother of Leonard Adams).

Second row (L to R): Roy Erdman, Mark Fetterolf, Donald Haas, Ernest Bensinger, Jay Erdman, and Guy Erdman.

Third row (L to R): Virginia Wetzel, Mae Martin (Paul's sister), Mae Fetterolf, Pauline Fetterolf, Alma Maurer (Lawrence's sister), Arlene Zimmerman, Elda Fetterolf, and Anna Fetterolf.

Clarence "Fetch" Fetterolf (teacher), Lawrence's first cousin.

Total 20 pupils.

The Fetterolf School, south of the Village off Hepler, was built on the Bensinger Farm located on Saw Mill Road, between Leonard Adams and Raymond Bensinger. The school was on the west side of the road and is removed today. This photo is courtesy of Lawrence Mauer, April 2006. Lawrence died in 2012. This photo is reproduced by his son, Ronald L. Maurer, of Halifax, Pennsylvania. Lawrence identifies the students in grades one through 8 and estimated the year to be 1930.

All the Fetterolf students named here are the children of Charles and Lottie Fetterolf. This family is described in the book *The German and Welsh Origins of the Charles and Lottie Fetterolf Family, Including Hodge, Reiner, Marsh, Kidson, and Skelding* by Steve E. and Joan E. Troutman, available from Sunbury Press. Pauline, named above, is Joan's mother.

CHAPTER 13

Delb/Delp School

Delb's School with the teacher's car. Notice the children playing in the yard and the old stacked rail fence behind the school. This photo courtesy of Mrs. Paul Klinger. Her husband, Paul Klinger, and his siblings all attended this school. The Paul Klinger farm is now owned by Eric and Kristy Klinger.

The Delp/Delb School served as the community center of worship for many years. According to the book *St. Michael's Lutheran and Reformed Church, 1894–1994*, this schoolhouse played an integral role in the establishment of St. Michael's Church in Klingerstown. Early records of Delp's Sunday School ledger, in 1868, tell us folks in the vicinity of the school were having Sunday School service and hymn sings at the building. At times, the attendance was around 100 people. Some names listed in the Delp's Sunday School records include officers, teachers, and scholars who are later named as officers in the organization of St. Michael's Church. Groups of people from nearby churches would attend Delp's Church School. A group of 30 people attending are named as visitors from Klinger's Church in Erdman.

The Former Delp School House. The current address is 1211 Old State Road, located near the intersection of Watershed Road and Old State Road, Upper Mahanoy Township, Northumberland Co, PA. This residence was earlier known as the Delp School. The Delp farm was on the intersection. This home was utilized as a house of worship in recent years. The top floor served as a sanctuary for a small Evangelical congregation. They referred to it as the 'Upper Room.'

In 1975, a box of books from the Delp's School was uncovered in the belfry of St. Michael's Church in Klingerstown. The oldest book was a Sunday School minute book with a beginning date of August 16, 1868. The record shows the attendance of 21 male and 16 female scholars, with 6 male and 6 female teachers. The last entry with remarks is on September 24, 1893. Fifty people attended the school. Rev. Kocher wrote, "The school will expire. All are sorry." A new church in the town of Klingerstown was built. Marcus Klinger, married to Elizabeth Delp, aided in the construction of this new house of worship. St. Michael's new Sunday School officers were elected on May 27, 1894.

Delb's School, 1928, A.M. Ressler, Teacher. Although the children are not named, this school was surrounded by families named Klinger, Mattern, Rebuck, and Strohecker.

CHAPTER 14

Zerfing's School

Zerfing's (District #2) schoolhouse is located just south of the late Walter Dietrich's home, on Hoffman Road, between Klingerstown and Rough and Ready, Upper Mahantongo Township, Schuylkill County, Pennsylvania. Herbert Snyder was the teacher.

Front row (L to R): John Starr, Dan Hoffman, Herbert Snyder (teacher), Albert Wolf, William Klinger, John Paul, Ida (Maurer) Wiest, Ruth Starr, Minnie (Romberger) Drumheller, Verna (Starr) Spotts, and Valera S. (Stiely) Malick.

Second row (L to R): Calir Hoffman, Edwin Knorr, Harry Erdman, Ray Starr, Carrie (Wiest) Brown, Carrie (Knerr) Herb, Gabriella (Wiest) Smeltz, Mae (Romberger) Rothermel, and Alfafa (Starr) Klinger.

Third row (L to R): Guy Starr, Allison Maurer, Gurney Klinger, Edwin Knorr, Wellington Maurer, Nevin Wiest, Jennie (Knorr) Paul, Maude Ellen (Stiely) Bossler, Gerie (Klinger) Klock, and Mima (Wiest) Rebuck.

Fourth row (L to R): Charles O. Starr, Herman Erdman, Sadie (Knorr) Diebert, Meda (Paul) Kessler, Minnie (Wiest) Starr, and Carrie (Erdman) Smeltz.

Fifth row (L to R): Charles Romberger, Walter Maurer, Wesley Wolf, Beulah Wehry, and Mazie (Wiest) Miller.

Zerfing's School, October 9, 1914, Upper Mahantongo Township, Schuylkill County, Pennsylvania. The children stand wtih the teacher as a group. Three rows were identified, although the rows are not straight.

Front row sitting (L to R): Bessie (Ramberger) Clark, Kathryn (Ramberger) Wiest, unknown girl, unknown boy.

Second row (L to R): Minnie (Ramberger) Drumheller, Raymond Ramberger, Kate Wiest, Emma Smith (small dark complexed child with a bow in her hair; George Deibert's mother), unknown girl with white buttons on dress, Helen (Ramberger) Davis, unkonwn girl with polka dot dress, unknown girl, tall unknown girl, Clarence Wiest (small boy with dark jacket), and Naomi, who was raised on Willie Erdman farm, which is now Mike Deibert farm, and married Charles Starr (standing next to her in back row).

Third row (L to R): Unknown boy, unknown girl with two riibbons in her hair and plaid shirt (probably a Hoffman), Annie Mae (Ramberger) Rothermel, Mary Starr (with black hair bow - married Howard Maurer), Erdman girl with black hair bow, teacher, Willie Klinger (nicknamed "Knickerty Knackerty"), Charles Starr, and unknown boy.

For more information on the Ramberger children identified in this photo, see the book *There is Something about Rough and Ready*, pages 107–115.

The newest one room school house in Rough and Ready is an Amish school. It is on the David Ray Stoltzfus farm. The school is located near the intersection of Range Road and Boyer Road. The public school system provides transportation for the Amish students. What was once old fashioned in our community, has now become the new norm for the Amish folks.

About the Authors

Although, 72 years old, **Steve** is in good health and retirement is not of interest. He enjoys making sausage and bologna which is sold at local farm markets. Steve, Joan, and his children, Michael and Valerie, all work in the family business, Troutman Brother's Inc. His great grandfather, Victor Troutman, established the butcher shop when the business was known as Victor Troutman and Sons. These sons later established the present business in 1929 renamed as Troutman Brothers. Steve attended Franklin and Marshall College and graduated with a degree in geology. Steve's grandfather, George, and parents, Earl and Marion, were historically minded individuals and passed on an interest in family history.

Joan and Steve at Troutman Brother's meat market, Klingerstown, Pennsylvania.

Joan was raised in rural Leck Kill in a farm family which did general farming. This included having chickens, beef, pigs, rabbits, two ducks, and of course, what every farm had, a large group of barn yard cats. The family also raised produce, including potatoes, cabbage, beans, sweet corn, tomatoes, cucumbers, water melons and cantaloupes. In the late spring, Clement bought strawberries from local farmers and often just took a truck load of strawberries to sell in neighboring coal mining towns. The growing, storage, and the bagging of potatoes were the farm's largest concern. Joan helped to harvest these crops which were labor intensive. She often states laughing, that the farm got a harvesting machine when she left to attend college! Joan graduated from Susquehanna University, with a degree in accounting, and now happily assumes front desk responsibilities at Troutman Brothers, Inc.

www.ingramcontent.com/pod-product-compliance
Lightning Source LLC
LaVergne TN
LVHW061346060426
835512LV00012B/2591